EMMAUS

the way of faith

STAGE 1: CONTACT

EMMAUS

the way of faith

STAGE 1: CONTACT

Connecting with people where they are

Stephen Cottrell, Steven Croft,
John Finney, Felicity Lawson and Robert Warren

Illustrations by Clare Parker

Second edition

 CHURCH HOUSE
PUBLISHING

Church House Publishing
Church House
Great Smith Street
London SW1P 3NZ

ISBN: 978-0-7151-4308-7

Second edition published 2003 by Church
House Publishing.

First edition published 1996 by The
National Society/Church House Publishing
and The Bible Society.

Acknowledgements

Scripture taken from the Holy Bible, New
International Version. Copyright © 1973, 1978,
1984 by International Bible Society. Used by
permission of Hodder & Stoughton Limited.
All rights reserved.

Cover design by Church House Publishing

Printed by Biddles Ltd, Guildford and King's Lynn

Contents

Preface

How do you get people to come on a nurture course? Most nurture courses assume a group is just sitting there ready to begin, but most churches find that getting non-churchgoers to join a group in the first place is the most demanding of tasks. What is more, if such courses are to bring people to faith it is also the most important.

This *Contact* booklet helps you to think through this key question. It can be used with any nurture course but is particularly designed for the *Emmaus* programme. You can read it straight through or use it as the basis for a four-session course for a church committee, a house group, a cell church, eldership etc. (see Chapter 10).

This second edition of the *Contact* booklet builds upon the experience of those who have used the *Emmaus* material since it was first published and also the considerable amount of statistical research into nurture courses which has been done in recent years.

Emmaus: the Way of Faith is a means of welcoming people into the Christian faith and the life of the Church. It is rooted in an understanding of evangelism, nurture and discipleship modelled on the example of Jesus as told in the story of the Emmaus Road.

Emmaus: the Way of Faith enables the Church to:

- Pattern its life around Christ's call to make disciples.
- Build relationships with those outside the Church.
- Accompany enquirers on their journey of faith.
- Bring new Christians to maturity.

Emmaus is about Luke 24 – Jesus walks alongside the two disciples, questions them, teaches them from the Bible and then thrillingly reveals himself to them. This booklet is about love – having such a concern for people that we are prepared to do something to help them.

Emmaus does not come from any single Christian tradition. It has been inspired by the recent renewal of interest in helping people to come to faith through following the pattern of Luke 24. It builds on recent research which has been done about nurture groups. It also looks back to what can be learned from the 'catechumenate' by which the Early Church prepared people for baptism. This 'accompanied journey' into faith is a process of enquiry, instruction and transformation as someone meets the living Christ through the witness of ordinary church members.

Emmaus comes in two formats: the main Emmaus course – a nurture course and four 'Growth books'; and also Youth Emmaus for those aged 12–17. This *Contact* booklet can be used with either.

Evangelism

There are three kinds of evangelism. Each has an unseen agenda which is very real but not immediately apparent!

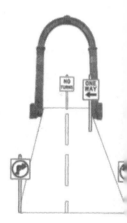

I 'Will you please come to my church?'

Hidden agenda: 'If you join our congregation we have lots of good things for you. Peace of mind, forgiveness of sins, fellowship: we also have an envelope scheme and the expectation that you will "join in" – and that will help *us*.'

2 'You will join in, whether you like it or not.'

Hidden agenda: 'Whether you want it or not I will *make* you a Christian. I will exploit your sense of guilt, your loneliness, your need for appreciation....'

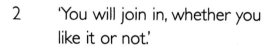

3 'Let us go together and see what God will do.'

Hidden agenda: I care for you as a person and want you to share what I have found... and much, much more.'

A nurture course like Emmaus is dedicated to the third way of evangelism.

To walk alongside another person as they come to faith is one of the most

■ faith-uplifting

■ life-enhancing

■ joy-making

things it is possible for a Christian to do. Evangelism helps the person you are making contact with. It also helps the person who is evangelizing: look at Luke 10 and see the effect that evangelism had on the disciples (vv. 17–20) – and the joy it brought to the heart of Christ (v. 21).

Therefore helping as many of the congregation as possible to evangelize is helping them to grow spiritually. They can help by:

■ *Inviting* people to the course.

■ *Praying* both in private and as a congregation (in the Services of Welcome; see *Emmaus: Nurture*, Second edition).

■ *Sponsoring* those on the course (see Chapter 8).

■ *Teaching* during the sessions.

■ *Welcoming* the new people.

If members of the congregation are not allowed to help with the course it deprives them of great spiritual benefit – it also locks away unused the gifts they can bring to others.

Putting the nurture course in the right place

Too many churches have 'bolt on' nurture courses. Usually these are the bright idea of the minister or a group of enthusiasts.

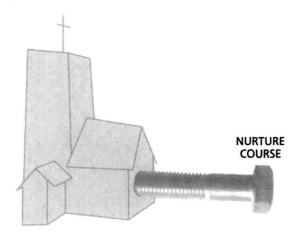

NURTURE COURSE

Such courses soon drop off the agenda – crowded out by other things.

Nurture courses are the proven best way to help people to faith and should be at the very heart of a church – even if it means the alteration or death of some existing activities. Sometimes there has to be a clearing of the decks so that the initiation of the new Christians is central to the life of the church.

The Early Church used the catechumenate to introduce people to the faith. It had all-age Sunday School during the main service and other weekly instruction on Christian faith, behaviour, prayer, etc. *for two or three years before the catechumens were baptized.* Work out how much time, prayer and energy must have been given to this process and put it alongside the efforts of your own church.

Do nurture courses work?

chapter 02

Christians need facts as well as faith. The Holy Spirit of truth teaches us to be realistic. Numbers can teach us lessons.

What does research teach us?

There have been several recent surveys (see list at end of chapter). They teach us:

Research note 1

People become Christians because of a relationship with Christians – and a nurture course provides an ideal opportunity to make friends as well as learn about the Christian faith.

> *So the openness and sincerity of the welcome and the pastoral care that is given are as important as the content of the meeting. Meals, outings and other opportunities for mixing people together all encourage this. Leaders can be tempted to concentrate so much on the content of the meeting that they forget how important the social side is.*

Research Note 2
People like nurture courses – a staggering 95 per cent said they found them 'helpful' or 'very helpful'.

> *So we should not be shy about asking people to come on them! If we don't we are denying them something which they will enjoy.*

Research Note 3

About one in six of those who come on a nurture course becomes a Christian. Over a million people in the UK have done a course so this means that over 200,000 have become Christians through such courses in the past ten years.

So a church that is not using nurture groups is failing to use one of the main ways in which God is working today.

Research Note 4
... but only one in three English churches runs a nurture group...

So opportunities are lost.

Research Note 5
... and nearly half give up after they have run only two or three courses.

So make them part of normal church life.

What happens when you run a course several times?

Nurture courses may appear to blaze in and then tail off. It is important to emphasize that this is a *short-term* effect. We need to understand the reasons why and to have a long-term picture.

Usually when a church starts a nurture group nearly all the members of the first course are the most enthusiastic church members and there are very few newcomers. They have a great time and the faith of those who come is much strengthened. But when they run a second course there are fewer church members and only one or two newcomers. Numbers are lower and the enthusiasm less. Often the same is true of the third course. But over 90 per cent of churches that persevere and run four courses or more report they have new Christians: they also report a definite upward trend in the size of their congregation.

Research Note 6
Virtually all churches which have a successful programme of nurture courses have some way of keeping course members in groups of one kind or another.

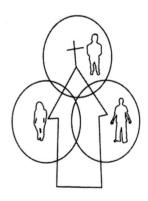

> *This is the whole idea behind Emmaus. It means that planning ahead for when the nurture course ends is vital.*

Research note 7
Most people (69 per cent) become Christians gradually – rather than having one datable experience of God (31 per cent). For some the experience is like a capital V– a sudden change, while for others it is more gradual like a U. This is true in all church traditions: even in evangelical churches the majority have a gradual experience – and a surprisingly high number (20 per cent) have sudden experience in non-evangelical churches!

> *So a nurture course should allow for different kinds of spiritual journeys and not expect everyone to go through the same pattern.*

Research Note 8

People found entry into church worship reasonably easy – if they came with a friend. This was true even of those who had never been to church before.

> *So leaders should make sure that new people are never expected to come to church by themselves. Nor should leaders be hesitant about inviting people to come for the aim is to make disciples who will continue in the fellowship.*

Research Note 9

Churches can grow. Twenty-two per cent of churches have grown by at least 120 per cent in the last ten years.

> *So decline is not inevitable and churches should not allow negative thinking to prevent evangelism.*

Therefore the first question is:

Should we have a nurture group?

(With the number of things going for it the real question may be, 'Can we afford **not** to have one?')

What do you need?

Faith

- That God will work through you. It does not depend on you.

- That God will bring people to a group. Ask him to bring those who should be there – and keep away those who should not.

- That God will touch them. If they are the right people then God has brought all of them for a purpose.

Chase away negative thinking.

Be positive! Pray about it with others.

- Learn all you can about groups and nurture groups in particular (but be careful of analysis paralysis). In particular read the other booklet in this series *Leading an Emmaus Group*.

■ Think how it could work in your situation.

The second question is:

How can we get a nurture group up and running?

Look at the *Introduction* of the Emmaus course for details of the procedures to be gone through.

In brief:

1   Explain, teach and persuade.

2   Make a decision to have an *Emmaus* course.

3   'Are we going to do it with others?' (some of the best courses have been run by several churches together – even covering a whole town or area)

4   'Who is going to lead?'

5   Make it happen:

    ■   Administration.

    ■   Prayer.

    ■   Encouragement: keep the vision before people.

6   Make space in the church programme to give the new infant space to breathe.

The third question is crucial:

How do we get people to come to nurture groups?

That is what the rest of this book is all about – *making contact.*

The statistics in this chapter come from various research sources: John Finney, *Finding Faith Today* (Bible Society, 1992); *Evangelical Alliance* (1998); Mark Ireland (MA dissertation, Cliff College 2000); *Religious Trends 3* (Christian Research, 2001); Charles Freebury (unpublished 2001/02); Robin Gill, *Churchgoing and Christian Ethics* (Cambridge University Press, 1999)

Every church has contacts

In old planes they yelled 'Contact' when the engine was about to be started. In churches we need to shout 'Contact' more often when people are going to start on their spiritual journey.

Most churches do not realize how many contacts they have. Every church has people who are in touch with other people in one way or another. We look at just five areas:

- Family.
- Occasionals.
- Special services.
- Others.
- Friends.

Family

Those who are connected through a member of their family: their child comes to a Cub pack linked with the Church... granny comes to church regularly – and her children and grandchildren live nearby.

Family contact can be three times the number in the congregation. So a church of 100 could have about 300 family contacts.

How many 'family' contacts does your church have?

Occasionals

- They come at Harvest and Christmas.
- They sometimes come to children's services.
- They come on the anniversary of a bereavement.

Experience shows that on average these are at least half the number in the congregation – therefore a church of 100 will have about 50 occasional attenders. Social background is important: the percentage will be higher in rural or suburban areas, lower in estates or the inner city. (One survey of 17 churches showed that while 620 adults were reported in church on an average Sunday, there were 1776 who came one a month.)

How many 'occasional' contacts does your church have?

Special services

- The average number of non-churchgoers at infant baptisms is 25.
- At weddings it is 80.
- At funerals it is 35.

Besides these there are parade services, school services, Remembrance Day services, civic occasions...

How many special service contacts has your church in a year?

People are nearly always amazed by the size of this number – it can be several thousand people in a busy church.

One church held a guest service. There were six new people: the minister was pleased. I asked him how many funerals and weddings he had taken that week... 'two funerals, two weddings'. At those services he had spoken to over 200 non-churchgoers: but they were just routine – not a wonderful opportunity to show the connection between the Christian faith and the life of ordinary people.

We need to brush up the way the Church conducts these 'chores of grace'.

Others

Let your imagination range.

How many people from the local community use your church hall?

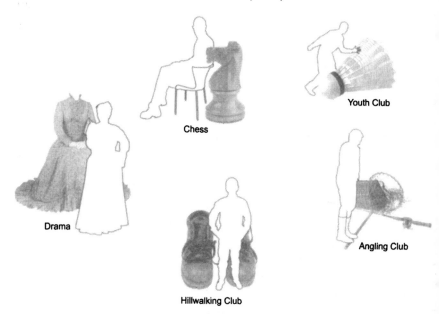

Chess

Youth Club

Drama

Angling Club

Hillwalking Club

How many do you contact in your social care of your neighbourhood?

Who gets literature from your church?

How many other contacts has your church?

Friends

Members of the congregation will have friends who do not go to church and who live locally. Allow for two such friends for each member of the congregation.

How many friends does your congregation have?

Add up the total number of contacts in each section:

Family	....
Occasionals	....
Special Services	....
Others	....
Friends	....
Total Number	....
But some people will be on more than one list, so divide by 2 to allow for duplication	....
Total number of contacts	....

Most churches will find this total very large – hundreds if not thousands: a sizeable percentage of the local population.

Begin where you are

It is sensible to start by evangelizing the people we are in contact with, rather than make special efforts to reach those we are not. Yet sometimes churches evangelize by trying to make yet more contacts through house-to-house visiting, etc. It may be a better use of effort to start at the beginning.

Belonging and believing

We have seen that a church has lots of contacts. But it is like a train journey where lots of people get off at the first station, more at the second and so on: very few reach the terminus of full Christian discipleship.

How can we help people to make the whole journey of faith?

We begin by belonging

One of the most important pieces of research in Chapter 2 showed that people come to faith through relationships.

Most people join a church and then find faith, rather than finding faith and then looking for a church to join (see next page).

Professor Robin Gill says: 'Belonging comes before believing' – not the other way round. This is very important for it is often thought that it is the opposite.

(There are exceptions but they are few.)

We should do all we can to help people to *belong* so that they can come to *believe*.

What is 'belonging to a church'?

Usually this is a social experience and it can be a spiritual one as well.

People do not have to attend Sunday services to feel that they belong:

- They may have a group of friends who go to church – and they begin to feel interested by what excites their friends.

- They may come to social events – and they begin to feel at home in the buildings.

- They may have had a good experience of a church at a family funeral or wedding. Often people find that they are touched at a time of great emotion, whether it is sorrow or happiness.

- They may meet the minister and find a human being. People expect a religious bureaucrat and find a real person who does not judge or intimidate.

If you asked them, they would say, 'St John's is my church'.

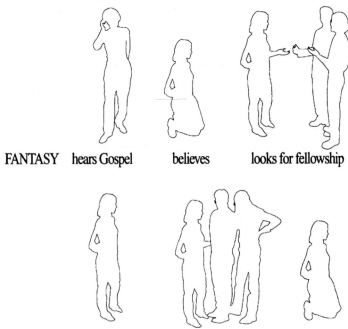

FANTASY   hears Gospel   believes   looks for fellowship

FACT   has contact with Christians   joins fellowship   believes

Your church – fortress or fuzzy?

Fortress churches have a definite boundary – you are either in or out. You have to do something definite to get in – go through a special service like adult baptism, solemnly sign a membership form, etc.

Fuzzy churches do not have clear boundaries. Some people are becoming part of the fellowship – others may be leaving. It is less easy to say who are the members.

Sociologists talk about 'bounded' and 'centred' sets. Fortress churches demand that you believe before you can belong – which research shows very seldom happens. In fact people find it easier to belong to a fuzzy church – but they can leave it more easily.

The best style of church is fuzzy – so that people can enter more easily – but there needs to be the challenge of Christian commitment once people feel that they belong. The best challenge is an invitation to join a nurture group so that people can find out what it is all about.

Experience shows that a high proportion of those who join a nurture group or catechumenate go on to commitment – and often show it by a public profession of faith such as baptism or confirmation. In a good group the social and the spiritual go hand in hand.

Let's take an example: Mary's journey

While this story refers to an individual, the model seems to be the common experience of many.

A series of episodes produces a pattern which leads to discipleship.

Church members see what Mary does. More important is the unseen spiritual journey she is taking. Each episode means a spiritual step for Mary.

Contact

Mary brings her baby to be 'christened' to the vicar of St John's.

Mary is frightened of going to the minister, but feels she should give her baby the best in life. The minister is surprisingly nice and suggests she starts praying for her baby.

The preparation and service mean little intellectually, but she senses the genuineness of the welcome.

She starts praying for her baby, and God becomes a little more real to her. The welcome makes her feel as though the church is 'hers'.

She is invited to join a mother and toddler group on Tuesday and comes. They are a nice bunch and she makes friends.

She finds the Church relevant to her needs. These are 'her' friends and they also see her baby as belonging to St John's.

She comes to church for a 'Pram service'. It is chaotic, but her sense of belonging widens. She enjoys it.

God is real. She is intrigued and begins to pray more. She buys a Children's Bible from the church bookstall – and reads it herself.

Mary comes to a children's service. She finds it strange, but fun. Her child is now aged two.

After a couple of visits the words in church begin to make sense, and she starts to look forward to the service.

She is asked to join an introductory meeting and then takes part in the full Emmaus Course.

She feels out of her depth, but knows she needs to follow it up. She makes close friends. Challenged, excited, happy, stretched, confused.

Commitment

Looking back, Mary knows that somewhere along this three-year journey she has become a committed Christian. Each episode has helped her to grow in faith.

As people come to Christ, most experience these episodes. In Mary's case it was fairly church-centred. But it does not have to be.

A faith-deepening episode can be:

■ A conversation with a friend which starts someone thinking.

■ A story from the Bible remembered from childhood.

■ A programme on the TV which makes someone start to wonder.

■ A beautiful view which shows a creator.

■ A dream which brings to the surface the desire for God (3 per cent of people say a dream was the most important factor in bringing them to God).

… almost anything that is significant.

chapter 05

What are they thinking?

Evangelism begins by loving and respecting people. So we have to be aware of what makes them tick.

Before we start thinking about the methods by which we can make contact with people we have to think about what is the agenda of the people we are contacting. We usually know all too well what our agenda is – to bring them to God through the grace of Christ – but we have to know what they are interested in. In this chapter we look at three areas that are important:

Being aware of their agenda

Christians talk too much!

Too often we don't listen to what the concerns of people are and then respond to them.

Too often we want people to hear our agenda – about sin and salvation and going to church and behaving as a Christian. If we do not listen we are not showing that person respect – in other words, we are not loving them in the name of Jesus. (Read the Emmaus story again in Luke 24 and notice how Jesus let Cleopas get all his feelings off his chest before starting to teach him.)

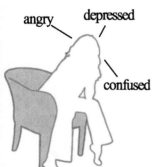

What is that recently bereaved woman saying?

'I feel angry.'

'I feel depressed.'

'I feel confused.'

If we don't listen, we shall not be able to help her. People in trouble loathe easy and glib answers that do not connect with their need.

When we talk to contacts we need to listen carefully.

What are those young parents concerned about?

- The mortgage.
- The wellbeing of their baby.
- Having a nice house.

But those may be only the obvious questions. Their real underlying problems may be:

- Insecurity ('Will I lose my job?').
- Confusion ('What sort of standards are we setting our child?').
- Relationships ('Will our marriage hold together?').
- Helplessness ('This is bigger than I can cope with.').

At the same time they may be discovering:

- New joys – in parenthood, building a nest.
- New responsibilities – and enjoying them.
- New contentment – in a settled home, a family.

As we listen to the contacts with one ear we need to use the other ear to listen to God:

'Lord, how can we touch these people for Christ?'
'Lord, what can we learn from these people?'

Being aware of their spiritual life

'I'm not religious, but I definitely believe in something.'

This quote from the remarkable research by Hay and Hunt sums up what many people think. They are not atheists, but they are not sure what they believe in.

It is often assumed by Christians that non-Christians do not have any sort of spiritual life. But this research shows that 76 per cent of the population say they have had at least one 'spiritual experience'. Further:

55% feel that their life has followed some sort of pattern.

38% have been aware of the presence of God.

37% have known prayer to be answered.

25% have been aware of an evil presence.

What is more there has been a marked rise in this spiritual awareness during recent years.

So when they talk about spirituality people may not have the right words to talk about it easily, but it is there all right.

Being aware of their social life

Only hermits do not live in communities. Every community has particular issues which are important.

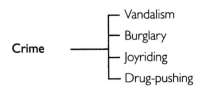

A caring church will share these concerns. Most churches will know what people's difficulties are through local gossip and newspapers (look at the letters page) but a quick survey can be revealing, asking:

- What most worries you about your neighbourhood?
- What would you like to see happen round here?

The church can work alongside community groups, local councillors, etc., to help in articulating concerns and doing something for the community. The process will bring you in close touch with many people who will see the church as 'getting stuck in'. Make it clear that this is gospel-driven – not just a bit of Lady Bountiful.

Building contacts

This section of the booklet looks at
particular areas where contacts can
be found. They are not theoretical
– they have been shown to work.

After you listen to people, don't
start doing something straight away.
There will be so many things that are
possible that a church can collapse
through exhaustion.

Pray and see what God wants.

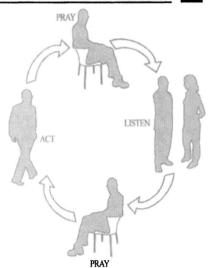

PRAY

LISTEN

ACT

PRAY

Contact I   Meeting their agenda

You may find that people need help:

■   To be good parents

Arrange a meeting. See who else would
back you (social workers, schools.) Get a
good speaker. Publicize the event to those
who would be interested.

■   To cope with debt

Talk to debt counsellors (Citizens' Advice
Bureau, etc.). Decide a course of action.
Do it.

■   To have a foundation
for their family

Gather a group of young parents to decide
what is most needed. Put it into operation.

■   To celebrate their happiness

Provide opportunities for rejoicing (church
services, parties, prayers on anniversary of
wedding, holidays together, etc.).

Don't concentrate only on problems. This may make people think God is a 'sticking plaster' – only good for emergencies.

Rejoice! We need to be able to celebrate and bring to God our deep happiness and the good things of life.

Show that God is interested in all of life

One woman said, before she became a Christian, 'God is an antique … out of date.'

We need to show that God is modern and concerned with people's real lives.

Example

A church started a church plant in a tough housing area. Twelve members agreed to get it going. After three years of hard work the number of attenders was – twelve. The church rethought the policy. A pub on the estate became vacant and they leased it. They asked the local people what they wanted it for, and helped them to get playgroups, a dominoes club, a keep-fit class, etc. going. Worship was restarted and soon the numbers leapt upwards.

Contact 2   Community groups

Many churches have contacts through groups which meet regularly. Often they represent one section of the community. Research shows that the most common are (in order):

1.   Parent and toddler groups.
2.   Senior citizens' groups.
3.   Women's groups.
4.   Men's groups.

Example

A church in a mixed middle-class and inner city area had two parent and toddler groups. Each had thirty parents (mainly mothers) who met on Monday and Wednesday mornings. The aim was to give 'the best mother and toddler provision possible'. The same Christian ran both groups with two teams of five helpers. All team members received training through the Pre-school Learning

Alliance programme and were able and trained to share their faith. They were also members of a Bible study group, and met monthly for prayer.

The parents were encouraged to join enquirers' groups. Partners were invited to an 'Open House' three times a year. Parents were invited to join the fifteen-week nurture course. At least twenty become Christians through this ministry in five years.

Research shows that almost all toddler groups where adults were becoming Christians had some sort of enquirers' group: it was not enough to expect church parents to witness at the meetings.

Example
A playgroup had a 30-minute evangelistic service once a term. As many of the children as possible took part through dressing up and processions. Mothers from Muslim and Hindu backgrounds came. Sometimes a church leader spoke, but it was found that the most effective testimony was that of a mother who belonged to the group.

Toddler groups meet two needs:

1. The need for children to meet and make friends.
2. The need for parents to meet and make friends.

In other words they meet the agenda of the people we are seeking to serve.

Other needs of young parents are:

- How to look after children properly – so have a series of parenting meetings.
- How to help their children spiritually – so have a gathering to talk about it (possibly linked with the parenting meetings).

Getting close to a group
Groups can become too big for friendship between the members and the leaders. Leaders can spend their time:

- Policing the youth club…
- Administering the men's group…

- Sorting out the Women's Bright Hour.

Leaders do not always have time to make relationships which lead on to enquirers' groups.

Example
The leaders of a youth club spent all their time trying to control the young people and protect the building. It was decided to close down the youth club and reform it as a series of 'A Teams'. Each team had two leaders who worked with their group to produce a six-week programme. The numbers of young people involved tripled, and far better relationships developed. A considerable number became Christians.

The principle behind this is applicable to many other groups:

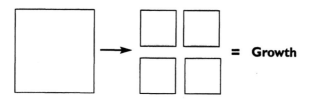 = **Growth**

Two kinds of contact

Although this booklet has concentrated on the contacts that churches already have, there are times when it is right to make contact through house-to-house visiting. There is no doubt that sometimes straightforward visiting can be helpful.

There are two kinds: **cold** and **warm**

Contact 3   Cold contact

People may respond to a street meeting for residents of an area on a local issue – vandalism, street lighting, facilities for pensioners, etc. These should be looked at practically but from a Christian point of view. Involve local councillors and social services.

Example

One church gave out a personal invitation to come to a meeting to address the issue of local crime, which a questionnaire had identified as the most prevalent local anxiety. Local police and probation officers spoke. Over fifty people came and were impressed by the church taking their concerns seriously – and some joined a nurture group subsequently as a result.

One particularly effective way of visiting the houses in an area is:

Prayer visiting

60 per cent of people pray – even more are glad when people pray for them.

Example

Three churches in a village worked together to 'prayer visit'.

A letter was delivered to each house in an area explaining that the churches were praying for the area. The letter stated that someone would call later to see if there was anything they wanted prayer for. Their streets would be prayed for the following Sunday, along with their requests (unless they asked for confidentiality).

When visited, nearly half had something they wanted prayed for. Only 10 per cent were not interested. The rest thought it was a good idea – many said it was good to see the churches working together.

Some of the prayer requests were general – world situations or intercessions about crime, etc. Many had requests for a sick relative or thanksgiving for recovery from an operation. Some people had very personal and heartfelt requests for themselves or those close to them: a Down syndrome daughter, a marriage in crisis, safe birth of a first grandchild, redundancy.

Often the visit led to long chats as people unburdened themselves or shared their happiness.

'Weep with those who weep and rejoice with those who rejoice.'

After eight rounds of visits, the three churches felt more confident, more united. Prayer visiting became a 'fundamental part of our ecumenical outreach'.

Prayer visiting shows that the Church:

- Cares for people who are not churchgoers.
- Believes in prayer and has a spiritual basis.
- Is not after your money (any gifts should be politely refused).

These are exactly the messages we want to get across.

Contact 4   Warm contact

This is visiting those with whom the church has some contact. It needs to be bathed in prayer and have a very definite purpose, preferably one that seeks to address the concerns of the people in the community. Inviting people to a single meeting is likely to be much more acceptable than asking them to join a course. Such a meeting can be in a school or local hall, but often it is best if it is in a house nearby. The meeting should address the issue in hand – but give an opportunity for people to go further if they wish.

Example
One church prayed through a list of all its contacts and decided to visit seventy-five homes with the question, 'Would you like to learn how to be a Christian in our town today? We shall be meeting in a house near you.' Over sixty people were interested and three nurture groups were started.

Contact 5   'Spirituality'

'God's important to me - I talk to him every day. And I'm, I wouldn't have said I'm a religious person.'

This quotation from Hay and Hunt's research well illustrates the 'religionless spirituality' which is so common today. For many people church or mosque or synagogue represents 'religion' which has little to say to their own spiritual life.

But often these people know their life of prayer is very thin and unfocused and needs to grow. Christians can do much to help – provided they are not seen to be representing 'church' and provided they do not appear to know all the answers.

Words that resonate with these sort of postmodern people are:

spiritual	colour
Celtic	life-enhancing
self-fulfilment	silence
creation . . . creativity	tactile
meditation	feelings
mystical	exploring
roots	paradox

Retreats, quiet days, even a fairly academic study of Christian mysticism in a local authority evening class have been attractive to these people who are finding the spiritual side of their being.

It has sometimes been found to be helpful if people are asked to pay towards the course.

Contact 6   Church literature

Many churches have literature which is widely distributed.

Whom are they addressing?

- Church people?
- Occasional attenders?
- Non-churchgoers?

Distribution lists show that magazines are often received by more non-churchgoers than churchgoers.

Is the magazine fit for them to read?

"Whenever I see a parish magazine, I tear it up before it can do any harm!"

What is the next step for such people?

Some people may respond to a directly evangelistic magazine, produced once or twice a year. This should include *an indication of how they can respond if they want to know more*. Remember the special offer – it may even teach people about the *free* grace of God.

Contact 7 Family services

These can be a useful entry point for the enquirer. A family service usually provides:

- Easier words and music.

- More to look at.

- Less demanding ideas.

- A more relaxed atmosphere.

It is often seen as a service primarily for children, with the children and their parents contributing to the service.

Useful research suggests:

- Family services only attract the 'fringe' when they are held **weekly** as the main service.

- Monthly services held at the usual service time attract very few, **unless** the monthly service is a 'Parade Service' attended by uniformed youth organizations. In such cases, a fair number of extra adults attend.

- If family services are held monthly *at a different time to the main service,* **a number of newcomers come.**

Family services which try to add on new people to an existing congregation that is used to a different style of worship do not usually work.

Family services do not have to be on a Sunday morning. Successful ones have been held:

- At 4 p.m. on Monday (children go with parents straight from school).

- At 5 p.m. on Sunday (followed by a tea).

- At 10 a.m. on Saturday (in the church school).

Research suggests that parents will come with their children a few times for the sake of their children. *However, if the adults continue to come, it is because they are finding it helpful for themselves.*

A new name?

Such services are often called 'family services', but do we have to use that name?

What does it say to

- The childless couple?
- The single mother?
- The divorced?
- The unmarried?

In fact use almost any other name!

Do we even have to use the word 'service'? 'Party' or 'celebration' might be more appropriate, as in 'a celebration of Holy Communion'.

Some churches call them:

Contact 8 Baptism

Infant Baptism

Health warning:
for paedobaptists only!

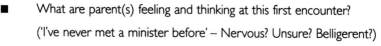

'Can you do our baby?'

This raises sub-questions for the church:

- What are parent(s) feeling and thinking at this first encounter?

  ('I've never met a minister before' – Nervous? Unsure? Belligerent?)

- Who are they most interested in?

  (Their baby!)

- What can the church offer which will make them feel comfortable?

  (People of their own age and interests, a welcome for them and their child, something that will help their needs.)

Research shows that the effect of a baptism was 'not so much what happened at the service but in the preparation beforehand and the follow-up afterwards' (see research in *Finding Faith Today*).

Example
A Midlands church asks couples to:

- *attend one discussion group*

- *attend church at least twice (a moderately 'high' and lively Anglican service) before fixing a date for the baptism.*

At the service the family are warmly welcomed (and photographed for a display in the church). Afterwards, parents are invited to join a group exploring the Christian faith.

About 20 per cent of parents become committed Christians, and a further 25 per cent begin to attend occasionally.

Contact 9 Marriage

Couples coming for marriage may be experiencing their first taste of church ever. What do they want?

- A smooth and happy wedding day.
- A touch of seriousness for a life-changing occasion.

A church wedding gives them all that (as well as a good setting for the photographs).

Some couples will want to bring God into it all – a meeting *after* the wedding for couples (and relatives) can be helpful:

- 'Let's think about the future.'
- 'Where do we go from here?'

This can lead on to an *Emmaus* course.

Divorcees

A church that will accept these couples (who are often cohabiting) will often find them open to faith. A welcome for those who are half-expecting rejection is all-important whatever the church policy is about remarriage of divorcees.

One church has found remarriage of divorcees to be one of their main evangelistic avenues. After the wedding many couples join an enquirers' group.

Contact 10 Funerals

All churches give pastoral care to the bereaved. Not all churches help them to move closer to God.

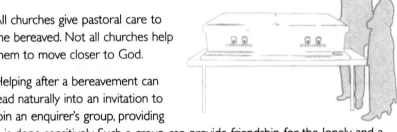

Helping after a bereavement can lead naturally into an invitation to join an enquirer's group, providing it is done sensitively. Such a group can provide friendship for the lonely and a chance to talk though the questions which bereavement has brought.

Some churches have developed groups where the bereaved can talk through their experiences in a relaxed atmosphere. One such group was called 'Picking Up the Pieces' and it gave much support to the bereaved and introduced them to the fellowship and friendship of the church: eventually quite a number came on a nurture course.

Contact 11 'Seeker services'

- Can we do without the jargon?
- Do people want to be known as 'seekers'?
- Are non-churchgoers attracted to a 'service'?
- Why not have 'Get-Togethers'?

These services are designed for the non-Christian. The flavour varies. According to the social context it can be like:

- A music-hall show with a compère.
- An event in a more 'refined' concert hall atmosphere.
- A pub sing-along.
- A performance in a theatre.

It has to be said that they are extremely time-consuming (and possibly expensive) to put on.

Experiences like the 'Rave in the Nave' services are definitely productive – possibly because they are addressing one particular sub-culture – that of young people (up to the age of about 25).

In each case the aim is to help people start to explore faith for themselves. There has to be something which enables those who come to go deeper into the faith or seeker services can simply be seen as a good night out. A nurture course such as Emmaus or Youth Emmaus is ideal follow-up material, provided that an introductory gathering is held first: many will be shy of committing themselves to a fifteen-session course.

Contact 12   Social events

All church gatherings are social events – but some are more social that others!

Barbecues, New Year parties, alternative Halloween parties, rambles, harvest suppers, garden fêtes, barn dances…the list is endless. Some raise money, some don't, but they all help people to meet. Often they include non-churchgoers.

Many people have a prejudice against 'church' and church people – these events help them to discover that Christians are 'normal' and enjoy having a good time. Contacts are made, friendships fostered. Beware of a toe-curling evangelistic slot at the end of the evening. Ensure that the Christians present act as hosts to the newcomers. Have a venue *slightly* too small for the numbers coming.

Often these events are more successful if they are organized by a cell church/ house group/ church organization rather than by the whole church. They are smaller, give responsibility to a small group, give a better opportunity for getting to know newcomers and enable follow-up to be more personal. However the group that organized it must be prepared to organize a nurture course for those who are interested in finding out more.

After the contact

The contact has been made. How do we get them there?

Publicize the enquirers' group widely:

through paper: posters, announcements, leaflets, magazine articles.

and especially

through people: there is no substitute for personal invitation – so ask, persuade, encourage, convince, plead. Remember that people need much reassurance before committing themselves to a nurture course. Nervousness comes from not being sure what is going to happen so explain in detail what the course entails. This is best done at an introductory 'no-commitment' meeting (see Chapter 9).

Above all **pray**

■ for the right people to respond;

■ for the right leadership to be given.

Then you will know that the people who came are those chosen by God – and he will not have brought them for nothing.

Get the whole congregation involved. Preach about it, encourage people to ask their neighbours. Have a 'Mission month' when this is the centre of the church's life.

When publicizing an Emmaus nurture course make clear:

■ Who it is for	Non-churchgoers, church people wanting a 'refresher', those wanting baptism or confirmation, newcomers to the church.
■ What it will cover	Is it just the intellectual basics of the Christian faith or what that faith can do in people's lives? Emmaus covers both.

- People can ask questions

  People are scared they will be talked at. Explain that questions are welcome – but it will be fine if they want to stay silent.

- What the end product is

  If the intention is that everyone should be baptized or confirmed, say so. If it is discovering where God is leading each person, make that plain.

Sponsors

The Emmaus story in Luke 24 is about one person walking alongside another.

Companions on the journey

A 'sponsor' is there to:

- Befriend someone coming to faith.
- Help them in any way possible.
- Pray for them constantly.

They need to be people who offer sensible, unpushy, friendship to others rather than expert Christians who know everything. They should be of the same sex, but do not have to be of the same age and background as the other.

helping hand

pray for

befriend

Helping others

The sponsor helps by:

- Showing the new person the way the church operates – explaining who does what, and why such-and-such happens.
- Introducing them to others in the congregation.
- Coming to the Emmaus course with the new person (and possibly helping to lead it).

The sponsor nearly always grows spiritually by helping in this way. An elderly lady who had acted as a sponsor said to one of us with tears in her eyes, 'I never thought God could use even me to help another.'

There is further information about sponsors in:

Introductory meeting

Before the Emmaus course begins it is helpful to have a meeting for those doing the course and their sponsors. It sets the tone of the course.

Meetings for non-churchgoers

When having gatherings for contacts:

1.	Have them well organized.	(We have a God of order.)
2.	Make sure a genuine welcome is given.	(We have a God of love.)
3.	Keep to the stated time.	(We have an honest God.)
4.	Do not have hidden agendas.	(We do not practise cunning – 'A gospel pill in a spoonful of jam.')

5. Invite people to only one or two meetings.

6. Have the gathering in a neutral setting where people can feel at ease.

- Pub
- Private house
- School

7. Explain on the publicity exactly what is going to happen and how long it is going to last

8. If there is a specifically Christian content – say so.

What to say to make sure they will never come back:

1. 'It is delightful to see you … I've been looking forward to meeting you all day.'

2. 'We feel the Lord has led us to begin these meetings'.

3. 'We'll start with a song - you may not know it…'

4. 'I wonder if you'd be interested in joining the Mothers' Union/our house group/the Christian Aid collectors…'

5. 'I went to the bingo/opera the other night' (whichever is culturally inappropriate).

6. Travelling mercies   church plant (cabbages?)
    Rite of election   New Wine
    Got saved   high church
    Deanery synod   cell church (prison?)
    Taizé   It says in Hezekiah …
    Spring Harvest   Toronto

… *and all other church language.*

After the introduction, the leader should emphasize:

- It is for beginners not experts – so ignorance is welcome!

- We shall start where they are, but will be talking about how God can help them.

- Everyone will come closer to God during this time and be touched by him. Change is normal and is to be welcomed – since it is change for the better!

- The course demands a high level of commitment – people need to mean business – but it is not serious and dull.

- Participants are free to drop out at any time.

- They don't have to contribute to discussions if they prefer to stay silent.

- They will need a copy of the Bible. It is useful for them all to have the same version and edition so that page numbers can be used.

- Arrange the date and time of at least the first two meetings. Make sure everyone knows where the meeting place is and how to get there.

- Begin praying for each other.

Using this booklet as a short course

The four sessions outlined can be used for:

- A church council or committee to get them thinking and talking.
- A group of church leaders to help them to do some lateral thinking.
- A house group that wants to think about evangelism practically.
- A group of potential or actual Emmaus group leaders.

These sessions can be used before embarking on an Emmaus group. However it has been found that it is often best used when the course has been run once or twice: it is then that the question of drawing in non-church members becomes most important (See Chapter 2 box, *What happens when you run a course several times?*).

While this is set out as a four-session course it can be shortened or lengthened at will.

session
[01 Evangelism and nurture

1 The nature of evangelism

Consider

p. 1   Which of these styles of evangelism fits your church?

p. 13   'Belonging comes before believing.' Is this your experience?

p. 15   How fuzzy is your church?

2 *The value of nurture courses like Emmaus*

pp. 4–8   This is the research. How far does it fit with your experience? What points are particularly relevant to your situation?

session 02   Journey into faith

1 *Stepping stones*

pp. 15–16   Look at Mary's journey of faith.

■   Get the sense of the growing awareness of God.

■   Feel the emotions she was going through.

■   Count the number of things and people that helped her.

Is she typical?

Have you or others had the same (or different) experiences of coming to faith?

Have you stepping stones for:

■   Young people?

■   The bereaved?

■   Divorcees?

■   Parents, etc., etc.?

Which can be 'episodes' to help them to faith?

2 *What contacts does your church have?*

pp. 9–12   What are your answers to these questions?

session
03 Contact

1 Look at the twelve examples of Contact on pp. 22–34.

■ Are you involved with any of these yourselves?

■ Are there additions you could provide?

■ Could they be used to produce contacts?

2 How can you listen to the agenda of the people around you so that you can follow through Contacts 1 and 2?

3 You now have:

■ The evidence for the value of nurture groups.

■ An indication of where to look for contacts.

Should your church embark on an Emmaus course?

(Have a time of prayer before deciding.)

session
04 Using Emmaus in your own church

1 Bolt on or central?

p. 3 Although courses are bound to be experimental at first, aim for them to be central to the life of your church from an early stage.

How can this be done?

2 Who?

How can you involve:

- The whole congregation?
- The church leadership?
- The potential course leaders?
- The church councils/committee?

3 What?

What needs to be done to make it all happen?

Prayer.

Administration.

> Communication – to whom?
>
> Training of leaders.
>
> Drawing together of first course.

4 When?

When is it all going to start?

Further reading

Ross Clifford, Philip Johnson and John Drane, *The Gods of the New Age*, Lion, 2001.

Stephen Cottrell and Steven Croft, *Travelling Well: A Companion Guide to the Christian Faith*, CHP, 2000.

Yvonne Craig, *Learning for Life: A Handbook of Adult Religious Education*, Mowbrays, 1994.

Steven Croft, *Ministry in Three Dimensions*, DLT, 1999.

Grace Davie, *Europe: The Exceptional Case*, DLT, 2002.

John Finney, *Finding Faith Today*, Bible Society/BCC, 1993.
    Stories of Faith, Bible Society, 1996.

Robin Gill, *Churchgoing and Christian Ethics*, Cambridge University Press, 1999.

Robin Greenwood, *Transforming Church: Liberating Structures*, SPCK, 2002.

David Hay and Kate Hunt, *Understanding the Spirituality of People who Don't Go to Church*, Nottingham, 2000.

Mission Theological Advisory Group, *The Search for Faith*, CHP, 1996.

Jenny Rogers, *Adults Learning*, Open University Press, 2001.

Francis Richter, *Gone but not Forgotten*, DLT, 1998.

General Synod of the Church of England, *On the Way: Towards an Integrated Approach to Christian Initiation*, CHP, 1995.

Robert Warren, *Building Missionary Congregations*, CHP, 1995.

(For other books and papers concerning statistical research see end of Chapter 2.)

The Emmaus web site is: www.e-mmaus.org.uk

The authors

Stephen Cottrell is a residentiary Canon of Peterborough Cathedral. Until recently he was a member of the Springboard Team and is a former Wakefield Diocesan Missioner. He is editor and co-author of *Follow Me*, a programme of Christian nurture based on the catechumenate, which is widely used by Anglo-Catholic churches. He has also written *Praying through Life*.

Steven Croft has been the Warden of Cranmer Hall within St John's College, Durham since 1996. He was the Vicar of Ovenden in Halifax for nine years. He is also the author of the handbooks *Growing New Christians* and *Making New Disciples*, and his work has pioneered understanding of the relationship between evangelism and nurture. His recent work includes *Ministry in Three Dimensions: Ordination and Leadership in the Local Church* and *Transforming Communities: re-imagining the Church for the 21st Century*.

John Finney was, until 1997, the Bishop of Pontefract and was also the Decade of Evangelism Officer for the Church of England. His report *Finding Faith Today* has been instrumental in helping the Church understand how people become Christians. He was also involved in the writing of *On the Way – Towards an Integrated Approach to Christian Initiation* for General Synod.

Felicity Lawson is Vicar of St Peter, Gildersome in the Diocese of Wakefield and is a former Dean of Ministry and DDO in that diocese. Together with John Finney, she wrote *Saints Alive!*, a nurture course helping Christians towards a deeper understanding of life in the Spirit.

Robert Warren was Team Rector of one of the largest and fastest growing churches in England, St Thomas, Crookes. He succeeded John Finney as one of the Church of England's National Officers for Evangelism and is now a full-time member of the Springboard Team. His book *Building Missionary Congregations* sees the catechumenate as one of the potential ways for facilitating the change required as we move from inherited patterns of church life towards the emerging models that will shape the Church in the next millennium.

Although all five authors are Anglicans, the Emmaus material can be used by any denomination and has been produced with this in mind.

Emmaus: The Way of Faith –
The Complete Resources

Introduction: 2nd edition
£4.95   0 7151 4963 6
Essential background to both the theology and practice of *Emmaus* and includes material on how to run the course in your own church.

Leading an Emmaus Group
£5.95   0 7151 4905 9
Straightforward and direct guide to leading both Nurture and Growth groups. It lays a biblical framework for group leadership, using Jesus as the example and model.

Contact: 2nd edition
£5.95   ISBN 0 7151 4995 4
Explores ways that your church can be involved in evangelism and outreach and make contact with those outside the Church.

Nurture: 2nd edition
£22.50   0 7151 4994 6
A 15-session course covering the basics of Christian life and faith.

Growth: Knowing God
£17.50   0 7151 4875 3
Four short courses for growing Christians: Living the Gospel; Knowing the Father; Knowing Jesus; and Come, Holy Spirit.

Growth: Growing as a Christian
£17.50   0 7151 4876 1
Five short courses for growing Christians: Growing in Prayer; Growing in the Scriptures; Being Church; Growing in Worship; and Life, Death and Christian Hope.

Growth: Christian Lifestyle
£15.00   0 7151 4877 X
Four short courses for growing Christians: Living Images; Overcoming Evil; Personal Identity; and Called into Life.

Growth: Your Kingdom Come
£15.00   0 7151 4904 0
This Growth book looks in depth at two main issues, the Beatitudes and the Kingdom.

Emmaus Bible Resources – Ideal for small groups!

Each book contains leader's guidelines, short prayers or meditations, a commentary, discussion questions and practical 'follow-on' activities.

The Lord is Risen!: Luke 24
Steven Croft
£7.95   0 7151 4971 7

Missionary Journeys, Missionary Church: Acts 13–20
Steven Croft
£7.95   0 7151 4972 5

A Rebellious Prophet: Jonah
Joy Tetley
£7.95   0 7151 4986 5

Christ our Life: Colossians
David Day
£7.95   0 7151 4987 3

Travelling Well: A Companion Guide to the Christian Faith
Stephen Cottrell and Steven Croft
£6.95   0 7151 4935 0

FOOTNOTE
If you would like to receive regular updates please join the *Emmaus* database.

Send your details to **Emmaus, Church House Publishing, Great Smith Street, London, SW1P 3NZ,**

email **emmaus@c-of-e.org.uk** or **call 020 7898 1451**.
The Emmaus website is at **www.e-mmaus.org.uk**